EPITAPH THEORY

HOW DO _YOU_ WANT TO BE REMEMBERED?

COREY SIGVALDASON

EPITAPH THEORY

HOW DO _YOU_ WANT TO BE REMEMBERED?

BY

COREY SIGVALDASON

© Copyright 2013 Outland Arts/ Corey Sigvaldason

Author's Website: http://www.epitaphtheory.com

Epitaph Theory Book site: www.outlandarts/epitaphtheory.htm

OLA3001   ISBN 978-0-9879642-5-0

First published March 2013

Printed in The United States of America

Published by

www.outlandarts.com
email info@outlandarts.com
1860 Lodgepole Drive
Kamloops, B.C. Canada
V1S IX8

Cover Illustration: "The Lesson" by William McAusland

Dedication

Dedicated to the memory of Brian Thomas Sigvaldason and Marilyn June Talarico, my father and mother.

Contents

Acknowledgements

I want to start by thanking God since it is only through his grace I have been able to put this book together. I am no model Christian but pray that he works with this man I am and helps me become the man I can be.

Mom and Dad

> This book was inspired by the lives of my mother and father. If it was not for their example and courage and guidance this book would have never been possible. Their lives prove the principles and teachings laid out in this book and how a legacy can grow through our influence while we are alive.

Angela

I also have to thank my wonderful wife Angela. She always believes in me and her encouragement keeps me going. She epitomizes the expression, "my better half." She makes all my efforts worthwhile and more enjoyable since I get to share it with someone I love so much. She is my angel on earth – my Angel-a.

Faith and Anna

My life and the meaning of legacy is complete with my daughters Faith and Anna. They bring meaning and perspective to everything and just looking into their big brown eyes and cute smiles lets me know anything is possible. I have found children truly bring priorities and meaning to life like no other.

Frank

I have been truly blessed to have grown up with two fathers in my life. My step-father, Frank Talarico, is the most amazing person I have ever met or heard of. Everyone that knows him respects him and he has never had an enemy in his life. He is an inspiration for his dedication, perseverance, faith, and knowing his priorities and values and always sticking to them. He is a model father and man and I count my self a tremendous success if I am able to become half the man he is.

Family

I am so fortunate to have a large family that loves and cares for me deeply. Their support has been a cornerstone of my life and I am so grateful to my brothers and sisters, uncles and aunts, and many cousins who not only put up with me but loved me even at my worst.

Those in the book (Kirk, Sue, Alvin, etc.)

I want to give a special thanks to those individuals, outside my family, whose influence and example made a tremendous impact in my life and this book. In particular I wish to thank Kirk Bathke, Sue Veillette, and Alvin Law.

Best Friends

Lynda Douglas and Kent Littleton – You both have been there in the good times and the bad. I am blessed to have you both in my life.

William McAusland

Motivator, great friend, and technology guru (layout and cover)

Outland Arts- Publisher

Shawn Wiesner-graphics

The graphics you see in the book I must thank Shawn Wiesner for. He is an amazing man whose love and commitment to family is an inspiration to many. He is a world class trainer and businessman who I feel lucky to call friend.

Interior Authors group

To all the members, past and present, of the Interior Authors Group. Their encouragement and accountability helped me persevere with this project and I thank all those talented individuals who believed in me and this book.

Many Others

To those in my life who touched me along the way, thanks for the difference you have made in my life and for the great memories. To all the others who encouraged me along the way I thank you. I hope you all enjoy this book and know you all play and part in its success.

Preface

I realize that talking about epitaphs, deaths, or just life on earth may be a topic that many, or most, prefer to avoid. However, I only use the reference as a graphic starting point that most can relate to. I realize that many believe that what we do on earth and focusing on our legacy may seem like an egotistical approach to gaining importance. For some that believe in life after death, this title and focus may seem misguided and off the real target. I agree that there are many things as important and some more important than our legacy. For instance, as a Christian I am taught that it is eternal life we are supposed to set as our goal. I know many other religions and faiths have similar approaches that go beyond the earthly realm and I want to make sure I respect that. I feel this book does address those other areas and feel that many of the stories and suggestions in fact compliment those various beliefs. My belief and desire is that each and every person who lives according to the principles in this book will not only leave a legacy but impact many lives along the way. In addition to your personal legacy and impact on others' lives, I desire the message in this book to positively affect any eternal consequences your actions may make.

I hope you enjoy the book and that it makes an impact in your life as this is part of my legacy and I want to ensure I am living by the principles I talk about. I would love to hear about any stories that relate to the book or how the book affected you.

God bless,

Corey

Quotes

Winston Churchill – "There comes a moment in everyone's life, a moment for which that person was born. That special opportunity, when he seizes it will fulfill his mission – a mission for which he is uniquely qualified. In that moment, he finds his greatness. It is his finest hour."

Jean Hudson – "Your life is your greatest gift. May you offer it in a service that fulfills you."

Mark Twain – "Live your life in such a way that even the undertaker cries at your funeral"

Michel Eyquem de Montaigne - "The value of life lies not in the length of days, but in the use we make of them: A man may live long, yet get little from life. Whether you find satisfaction in life depends not on your tale of years, but on your will."

Thomas Campbell - "To live in hearts we leave behind is not to die"

My Dad – "Live to love, love to live" (His Epitaph)

Lynda Douglas – "I told you I was Sick"

Introduction

You are dead! Now you ask yourself these questions: Did I live wisely? What attitudes got me to where I am today? Did I forgive enough? Did I love well? Did I serve greatly? Did I matter to this world?

Most people wait till the end of their lives to ask these questions. Or worse yet, someone else asks and answers them at their graveside. I say live every day as if you are writing your own epitaph. Don't wait to find out the meaning of your life till you are at the end.

We are busy. We go about our lives and business without pausing to think of our impact. Our actions not only change our lives but also have a profound impact on others, usually without us knowing it. People may not remember what we said but they do remember what we did and how we did it. *How do you want to be remembered?*

This book is about writing the tale of your own life. Writing your story the way you want your life to turn out. It is about finding your heart's desire and the difference you hope to make in this world as a result of the person you are and who you will become. This book is about creating your legacy.

Our time on earth is finite yet we allow ourselves to get caught up in the rat race called life. We are keeping up with the neighbours or our friends, or if 'we are lucky' we are getting ahead. What the heck are we trying to get ahead of I ask? We are trying to meet social expectations and the pressures that the outside world puts on our inner world. We don't slow down, smell the roses, watch the sun come up, dance with our kids and marvel in the small things that bless our lives every day. We are on a continuous quest to chase all those small things we can get in our lives

- the stuff – material possessions, power, promotions, prestige, admiration and the envy of others. We may have conquered the highest mountains but have we mastered ourselves? Our minds are being stretched daily but our lives seem empty and unfulfilled. We feel something is missing so we seek *things* to mask emptiness. This perpetuates the cycle and feeds the void.

Robin Sharma in his book <u>Who Will Cry When You Die</u> provides the following advice:

> "Do not wait until you are on your deathbed to realize the meaning of life and the precious role you have to play within it. All too often, people attempt to live their lives backwards: they spend their days striving to get the things that will make them happy rather than having the wisdom to realize that happiness is not a place you reach but a state you create. Happiness and a life of deep fulfillment come when you commit yourself, from the very core of your soul, to spending your highest human talents on a purpose that makes a difference in others lives. When the clutter is stripped away from your life, its true meaning will become clear: *to live*

for something more than yourself. Stated simply, the purpose of life is a life of purpose."

"Someone once said to me that the first fifty years of life are dedicated to building one's legitimacy while the last fifty are devoted to building one's legacy.... Many of us spend the first half of our lives striving for achievement and struggling to gain respect. Once we have this legitimacy, whether it comes in the form of prestige or material possessions, we soon realize that something is missing. We then spend the remaining years of our lives trying to do what we should have done from the beginning: Create a Legacy (1)."

How do you "create a legacy"? It starts each day with you as if it is the only day you have. What would you do with it?

When the answer to that question is based on life vision it brings clarity to your priorities. When you have this clarity, you carry within you the motivation to accomplish anything your heart desires.

You conduct your life with integrity and leave your imprint by helping others. You make the *shift from chasing success to creating significance.* This leads to manifesting your heart's desire in the outside world while being fulfilled in your inner world. It ultimately brings you to the realization of your true potential and your growth from goodness to greatness.

Once you are living a life of purpose, success and failure become only results. Your daily life gives greater meaning to successes and turns failures into momentary setbacks. These setbacks become more bearable because you journey with integrity when you are led by a purpose. As a result, your life has meaning and you leave an everlasting impact and impression on the world. The world is a better place because you were part of it.

Think of the impact your goals will have on others. Work hard to achieve them. Do not care what neighbours think but care about what loved ones think and the impact of your goals and actions on them. More importantly, think of the impact on yourself and the ripple effect you can have in this wonderful world we live in. Success isn't about getting more or doing more, it is about being more.

"Begin with the end in mind" is the phrase Stephen Covey made famous in his best selling book <u>The Seven Habits of Highly Effective People</u>. In Epitaph Theory, I have you look to the end of your life and work backwards while moving forward to your beautiful future. In the process, my desire for you is that you live your life like you are writing the epitaph on your tombstone and how you want to be remembered.

Real and lasting happiness comes through the progressive accumulation of loving memories and special moments. When I die I would rather people say I made time for them, served them well, and that my love and generosity was overflowing. Instead of asking, "How can I have more?" The real question becomes, "How can I be more?" Life will have challenges and lessons. No one said it was going to be easy. Rather than wishing for fewer problems in your life, I challenge you to wish for greater wisdom, strength, courage, and faith to carry you through what life brings your way.

At the beginning of each day, to keep on track and focused as you build your epitaph-worthy life, ask yourself these questions. How would I live this day if I knew it was my last? What do I have to be grateful for in my life? Even though we are never given a deadline for our time on Earth, we know we can't live forever. Everyone is given a finite time to accomplish their goals, dreams and visions. However our legacy and impact on the world lasts forever.

Chapter 1
The Power of Words

In the headlong rush through life and race for success we can miss the power of our words and the impact they have on others and ourselves. We come into this world not knowing the rules of communication. We cry or scream when we need something. We smile or laugh when we are happy. As we grow we learn words, then phrases and sentences. Our parents take delight in our emerging skill. We can talk! We are now communicators. And what comes out of our mouths from then on has a huge impact on others as well as ourselves.

You have seen people who go through life without recognizing the impact of what they have to say. This seems to be the case with people who use words to frighten, belittle, and shame others and themselves. Might you be one of those people? Let's pause here and see if you need to take a fresh look at what comes out of your mouth.

Our words have the power to do good or to do bad. Which do you choose? Do you say things without thinking of the consequences?

As a youngster you may have called someone a nasty name: fatty, shorty, stupid, wimp, loser, nerd, geek, or cripple. Those words can inflict a lifetime of pain.

What would happen if we used our words and actions to do good? What if you went up to an overweight child on the playground and told them you wanted to play. Can you imagine the potential impact?

What if a student was struggling and feeling it may not be worth continuing in school and wanting to quit? That student may simply need to hear words of encouragement from his or her teacher. What if that teacher said, "I can tell that you know the material and have the potential to be the smartest in the class. What can I do to help get you there?"

These experiences actually happened to me. In grade ten my teacher changed the course of my life and she changed how I thought. She gave me hope and spurred me on to be so much more than I was demonstrating at the time. I will never forget Mrs. Veillette.

Alvin Law also experienced how the power of words hurt and devalue as well as support and open doors. Alvin was born with no arms. He tells the story of people who had an impact on him, both positively and negatively. A piano teacher told him he could never play the piano since he had no arms and even though he learned to play with his feet (or as he called them

– his hands) the teacher told him his toes were too fat to play. Alvin stopped playing piano.

Years later a high school teacher told him and his parents he scored the highest on a test for musical aptitude. This teacher gave him the opportunity and tools to go on to become a celebrated jazz musician. Today, Alvin plays many different instruments such as: the trombone, the drums, piano and keyboards and uses his story and music to illustrate the impact our words and actions can have. Alvin's story beautifully illustrates the enormous impact that other people's words—positive and negative—can have on the unfolding of our lives.

We are given a choice each and every time we open our mouths. We have learned to communicate; now, what are you going to do with it? Choose your words carefully. You can never know the impact of your language and words. Choose to empower people with what you say. Sometimes even the simplest and seemingly meaningless things we say or do have an impact. Choose to build not destroy.

Think of times in your life when you have been affected by the power of words. It may have been something very powerful and good or it may have been something that has led to a deep hurt you still carry with you. Are you repeating the same language that has hurt or stifled you into thinking small or that you are not good enough?

We do it to ourselves as well. We can fill our self-talk with mean-spirited criticism and nagging. What would the world look like and what could be accomplished if we changed our language? Instead of saying, "I'm not, I can't, I won't," we re-shape our language to empower us and start speaking the language of leadership which says "I am, I can, and I will."

Are you looking for a promotion at work? What do you say to yourself right now when you think about it? It may be something like: "I'm not going to get that promotion. There are other people who will get it first. I don't get the recognition I deserve". How would your attitude at work change if you modified the wording:

"I'm going to work hard and stand out so I get the recognition I deserve. When the promotion comes along, I'm going to have proven my worth and get that position."

Just by shifting our self-talk we empower ourselves rather than becoming a victim of self-sabotage. Rather than deciding that something is not going to happen, think of how it can happen. How? Using positive language will develop a positive attitude and keep you moving toward your goals. Just by reframing the old word, you take back the personal power you were giving up.

Our discussion about the power of words would be incomplete, without including the three most powerful words in any language: I love you! These words have saved lives, transformed nations and changed the world in so many ways. Never take these powerful words for granted. They are more than mere words. Their meaning is deeper than just eight letters in a certain sequence. They are the universal language.

Some say "stick and stones may break my bones, but words will never hurt me." I say sticks and stones may break my bones, but words can kill me. I believe that is why we see suicide in the world. Some people had the power of words destroy them rather than build them. Words have far more power than anything on this earth. Choose them wisely. Make your words count. We can all make a difference and leave a legacy by saying and sharing something good.

You may never know the impact you have left on someone's heart through your words. And you may never know the legacy you are leaving by being verbally supportive of others. What I do know is you can choose a life of purposeful joy and, as a result, leave both a positive impact and meaningful legacy. I challenge you to go forth and speak the language of love and empowerment. It is a gift to others and, more importantly, it is a gift to yourself.

Chapter 2
Success: Is Your Ladder Of Success Leaning Against The Right Wall?

So "What is success?" You ask. Are we not already successful?

Have you been told that if you want to be the best in your profession, you need to duplicate what the person you admire most is doing? You need to look like, do the same things in the same manner, and 'be that person' or 'fake it till you make it.' Yuck!

I believe that if you want to excel in your work, personal life, or relationships, whatever it is, you need to be yourself. You need to be happy with the person you see looking back at you in the mirror. You need to be you, not somebody else.

People are perceptive if you are not being yourself. If you are acting, they will know. What makes one person successful does not necessarily make success of another. Everyone will define success in their own way. We need our individuality. We need to be true to ourselves. Seek success within yourself first.

How do you know when you have succeeded? How do you measure success? Is it money, power, prestige, status, or having lots of stuff? For some it is being able to walk, living another six months, waking up, having someone to love, or being able to have kids. When success is our legacy, it may unfold after we are here to measure it.

Terry Fox set out to raise $25 million for cancer research. He planned to run across Canada and raise $1 for every Canadian. Terry did not make it. The recurring cancer took him off the road and into the hospital and, sadly, took his life, his run uncompleted. Then what happened? Terry's legacy stayed on the road. It still lives on. His success continues to grow even after he is gone. The annual Terry Fox Run has raised over $550 million now. It will raise plenty more when great grandmothers are telling the story of seeing flags flying half mast from one end of the country to the other.

Terry also keeps inspiring others to make a difference. The legacy ripples out through people like his close friend Rick Hansen. Rick's "Man In Motion" tour wheeled around the world. That tour raised money for people with disabilities, or, as I like to say, people with different abilities. Rick, still active in raising money and awareness, will leave his own, unique legacy, as he follows his inner voice.

Success and failure are only results. You need not get caught up in either. The famous sales guru, Tom Hopkins said, "Success is a journey, not a destination." I say, "Success comes not from the journey but how you travel."

So now I ask you the questions: ***What is important to you?*** What are your priorities?"

I will be the first to admit we can lose sight of our life purpose, even once we have found it. This happened to me with my first wife when she was in the hospital just after we got married. She arrived in her room after having her ovaries removed due to a massive cyst that could have killed her. She was devastated. This would be devastating for any woman but even more so since she was in her early twenties at the time. I was in her room when she returned from surgery. It was filled with flowers and stuffed animals. My reaction, sad to say, was that my gift had to be the best. Up to that point, I hadn't even thought to get her a gift. Now I was a man on a mission. I knew how to handle this. I spent the next eight hours… the entire day… looking for the biggest stuffed animal I could find. In retrospect, I was the big, dumb animal. Rather than just being there for her in her time of need I let my ego take over. The only things she wanted and needed from me, my time and attention, I didn't give her. I can now see the pain of the situation sent me careening off, away from a life purpose to be proud of.

On the other hand, trauma can serve to clarify our priorities. During the terrorists' attacks on September 11th, 2001, many people called home to tell their loved ones how much they mattered and how much they were loved.

My trauma clarification happened on October 31, 1994. My step-dad called me after the hospital called him to say my mother had been in a terrible accident. At the time, my family was fractured and relations among us were strained. However, when mom arrived at Royal Inland Hospital emergency covered in blood, my family's priorities changed. As I stood at the end of her bed, if the sight of her broken body weren't enough, we then watched helplessly while she was losing consciousness and stopped breathing. My mother was dying.

The problems we faced prior to that moment disappeared and I just wanted the opportunity to tell her I loved her one last time. The horror of realizing that opportunity was slipping away from me filled me with fear and sadness. If only... why hadn't I just.... The shameful regret of life opportunities lost. Forever, the helpless horror of not being able to do a thing about it.

Thankfully, I got that opportunity to say all those things I worried about never getting the opportunity to say but now my mother was a quadriplegic.

During my research for this book I asked many people for their definition of success. The definitions were as unique as the people providing them. My mom defines success as "how good you feel about yourself." She says it is measured many different ways based on your life experiences. For her, it is "Getting through the day on a positive note, not dwelling on the past, and looking to the future positively!" She continues on to say she feels fortunate because she has her husband and children. She is never lonely and always feels loved and supported. What really touched my heart and made me think was her final comment. "If I get down, I just think of others who are worse off." Many of us cannot imagine being worse off than a quadriplegic and here is a quadriplegic who gains strength from the perspective that she is blessed with what she has and it could be worse. I am so proud that I have such a great role model and am loved and have learned lessons I can pass forward to my own family.

Robin Sharma describes success—real success, success that matters, success that is worthy of a legacy. He outlines what success isn't.

> "For you to win, no one needs to lose…. But striving to beat the competition breeds tremendous stress-you fall into the performance trap and begin thinking that you'll only

be admired if you win…. We become obsessed with outperforming others. We become like circus animals, performing in the hope of receiving acclaim from others. We base our self-worth on receiving praise from those we care about and, therefore, we keep pushing ourselves relentlessly. But nothing can ever be enough if we live like this(1). "

How do you build success? Focus on being the best that *you* can be. Never compromise your priorities and you will live a life of integrity which is critical to happiness and success. Be true to yourself. Judge the value of a person by their heart and strength of character not the size of their wallet or their material possessions. Think of all the riches you already have in your life: The love, the relationships, the beauty of the sky, the sun, the dandelion in the pavement crack. This will make the answer to the question "Are we not successful already?" an easy one. You are very successful already!

Chapter 3
Vision

"The Most pathetic person in the world is someone who has sight, but has no vision."
Helen Keller

Having a powerful vision that guides you empowers you. All the greatest leaders and business people start with a great vision. It is core to any business. One story of a great vision is the Jardine Family who took their little sports store in Kamloops to a national franchise called "National Sport Mart". That vision guided them to many riches and left a positive legacy for the city in which they started.

One vision I had was being a boxer like in the Rocky movies I enjoyed while growing up. When I finished high school I started boxing but never really got into any meaningful competition. I would always come home with either a black eye or cut on my face and almost always had blood on the front of my shirt I worked out in... more often than not it was my own.

My wife hated that I continued this boyhood dream and on many occasions asked me to stop. Then my opportunity came. Kamloops was going to host a toughman competition.

This was my shot in front of the home town crowd. I trained hard for 6 months. Believe it or not I got down to a ripped 165 pounds. As the day came closer and closer so did the realization of what I was going to do. What was I thinking? My first goal was now just to show up at the competition. I was in the first bout of the evening against a guy I had met in my gym who had competed in toughman competitions before. People almost laughed after every introduction when they would talk about credentials and number of fights... mine was very short since this was my first and only boxing competition outside my club.

At the end of the first fight I had won by a knockout in the 2nd round. I survived and that was all that really mattered... until I realized I had to keep fighting. That meant I went into the semi-finals against a competitive kickboxer from town who had been fighting for years – Mark Hartell.

I was so scared and worried. Apparently fear can be a great motivator since I went on to win that fight and qualified for the finals. Yippee! Only problem was it was against a guy who had 185 amateur fights, was a Canadian champion, and a carded Olympian.

Now I knew what fear really was. I got in the ring and started to fight but had a hard time catching the guy. I would swing and miss and he would stick out one of those large arms on his 6' body and put it right in my nose.

This went on for the entire first round. Then the bell rang for the second round. I decided I needed to start fast and surprise him. I threw a straight right at his head but he moved and it hit him in the shoulder. I saw his shoulder pop out of its socket. Everyone in the university gymnasium that night went "OOOOHHHH!"

His corner and the doctor worked on him for about a minute and then it happened... his shoulder popped back into place. He rolled his shoulder around a bit and came back out to fight. I was so scared at that moment all I wanted to do was go the distance with this mad man without being knocked out. Although I got 3 standing eight counts, I never saw the canvas. I managed to make it the distance. Just like in the first Rocky.

I knew I had realized my vision when I went back to the gym the next night and everyone cheered for me... many actually calling me Rocky for how I performed. To tell you the truth I am glad that vision has been realized and hope you all find visions that are far less painful.

In my work I meet many people with vision and passion to get into business. What I have found is those individuals that do the best in business are those with a clear purpose and vision for their business. In the business plan workshops our company provides we talk about vision in the first session since it is the guide for what the business will become and sets the tone for everything else that is taught afterwards. Vision in a business is about the values a company holds and what they ultimately hope to accomplish. I could write an entire book on vision in business, and someday I may do that, but for today I want to emphasize that in business, like in life, those with a great vision are more confident, productive, focused, determined, and are more effective than those that lack vision.

It is not enough just to have vision. The vision has to be one that comes from within and truly inspires you. I haven't always lived this principle and remember a time back on April 17, 2002 where I realized my own incongruence with a vision that was not mine. I realized that many of the goals I had set in business I did not "honestly" believe in because they were set or influenced by others and their expectations or experience. When we try to live out someone else's vision we sabotage ourselves with self-doubt. The disconnect creates enough space for doubt to work its way into our thoughts. However, *when you believe in the dream, that's when you are given the power to accomplish it.* I challenge you to dig deep and come up with your very own vision.

A great example of how we can never accomplish much by always following someone else's vision is the story of a man named Steve Fonyo. Steve was a man who lost his leg to cancer and was inspired by Terry Fox's vision of running across Canada to raise money for cancer research. I will come back to Steve's story but first I will expand on what I told you earlier about Terry Fox.

Terry Fox's goal was to raise $1 per Canadian by running the equivalent of a marathon a day across Canada, starting in Newfoundland and finishing in Victoria. Terry Fox surpassed his goal of raising a $1 per Canadian but was unable to finish his Marathon of Hope. He was struck by cancer again and finished his marathon in Thunder Bay before going home to be with family. Terry did not accomplish the vision as he originally planned it. However, he reached his goal, the reason he was running across Canada in the first place, of raising more than $1 per Canadian for Cancer research.

Terry's legacy lives on every September in the annual Terry Fox run held across Canada. His vision is truly inspiring and he has far surpassed his original goals. Terry Fox's legacy keeps growing.

Steve Fonyo, a young man from Vernon, B.C., decided he would also try to run across Canada and raise money for cancer research years after Terry Fox had set the original vision. Amazingly, and to his credit, Steve Fonyo made it from coast to coast and dipped his leg in the ocean in Victoria, B.C. to mark the end of his journey. Despite doing something Terry Fox did not do (successfully run across Canada), Steve Fonyo, did not come close to raising the money of Terry Fox. It was not his vision and people knew it. I remember hearing people talk about how he was doing it just for popularity, an assumption I find utterly absurd. However, it points to one of the pitfalls of following someone else's vision, even when you improve on it.

A great vision inspires others.

Often the vision you set does not get realized until long after you are gone. I think back to Martin Luther King's "I Have A Dream" speech. His vision was not realized until many years later and is still being battled for.

People with visions like this, the greatest leaders, are lonely at first. They run into criticism and it is tough. However, their vision is stronger than all that. They believe in the vision and not even the threat of violence or death deters them. The best leaders throughout history were driven by a purpose beyond their lives. It is what makes them great leaders – They create vision where there was no vision before. The state of your life, happiness, family, and business is determined by your vision. Remember vision is never limited by circumstances. Vision rises above circumstance.

Dream the dream. What inspires you most. Ask the question, "How can I make a difference?" It is a funny thing how when we often ask the right questions we are given the answers.

Robin Sharma in <u>The Saint, The Surfer, and The CEO</u> says this:

> "Most businesses have it all wrong. The goal isn't to make money. It is to make meaning. *Good companies focus purely on profit. Great companies focus on their higher purpose – to create great results for their customers and make a difference in their lives.*"

With vision you shift from "success chasing" to creating significance. This leads to the realization of your true potential and your growth from goodness to greatness.

The best leaders throughout history were driven by a purpose beyond their lives and higher in purpose than their lives. It is what makes them great leaders – they create vision where there was no vision before.

J.C. Penney, when he was in his 90's, said: "My eyesight may be fading but my vision has never been better"

Henry David Thoreau: "If you advance confidently in the direction of your dreams and endeavour to live the life you have imagined, you meet with success at the most unexpected times."

Leo Tolstoy: "Life is short. Do not forget about the most important things in life, living for other people and doing good for them."

Chapter 4
Values and Authenticity

What are your unique gifts?

When you are true to yourself and live authentically, you develop what is called *'attraction capacity.'* People like you for you. I know when I am my authentic self I am at my best and feel the most inner peace. Often we assume that people have expectations of us and we then act in ways we assume they want us to act. I am always reminded of the expression that goes with the word 'assume' – it make an *ASS* out of *U* and *ME*. I don't necessarily agree with that, or at the least the way it is said and written. I think it only makes the person who assumes the one who looks bad. Stephen Covey puts it this way, "Seek first to understand, then to be understood." Put another way, "To be more interesting you need to be more interested." Those are great words to live by.

No one likes someone who is fake or not genuine. We can smell the stench of fakeness and lack of authenticity. We typically see, hear, and smell them coming. More often than not these are the people who are loud, obnoxious, showing or telling you about their latest purchase or accomplishment, or they are quick to gossip or put others down.

When we live our authentic life, we carry the power to live our life without regret. I know there are times when I will not be totally authentic and that is okay. It is through our awareness and sensitivity that we can change and journey more closely to our most authentic life on a consistent basis. The start of our awareness comes from the realization that we no longer need to prove our worth. We can let go of the pressures of manipulative gestures or falsely manufacturing it since when we are authentic it just shows and we see it because it is mirrored back to us in the people around us. One of my coaches, Richard Burley from Calgary, put it this way:

> "Authenticity is a personal leadership imperative. It is not an internal expression but an external expression of others that appreciates in value. It is a visible reflection of who we are in the eyes of others. It can be subtle. It can simply be the authentic joy in your child's eyes when they see you walk in the door at the end of the day."

The purpose of life really is a life a purpose. However, if you plan on adding value to the world and provide a significant contribution, you must first know who you are. Being authentic means knowing where you stand and where you stand on issues. It is about consistency, not about being right or wrong, embarrassed or proud, success or failure. It is about being able to look in the mirror and be happy with the person you see looking back at you. Only when you know who you are and then be your authentic self will your beauty shine and your purpose become clear. It is when we have this clarity that we begin our journey to mastery.

Enjoy the journey but realize when you arrive that you have always been there. Authenticity unravels the riches below and your beauty shines like gold in the flowing river we call life.

I grew up in a household with my mother and stepfather and three half-sisters. Many of the values I have today come from my stepfather. Many believe, as I do, that he is an angel on earth. What everyone knows who has ever met him and spent time with him is he is the most authentic individual you may ever meet. This remarkable man has the love and respect of all those that he comes in contact with. He has no enemies and never has. His success and what people admire most about him is his undying devotion to his core values. When his values get tested, and believe me they have been, his values get strengthened and he inspires others by his focus on what is truly important and what he values most.

When most people would give up, Frank Talarico is battling on and strengthening his beliefs and values. This is what authenticity is about – being true to oneself. Authenticity is about knowing your values, priorities and beliefs and standing on them, even when they may not be popular or understood.

Ask yourself these questions: *Where did I come from? What has this taught me?* Many people shape and mould our lives and their influence shows. We reflect where we are from and the lessons we have learned from those that touched our hearts. We may be a lot like someone else but we are still unique and it does not make us any less authentic. A great example of this is when we hear the comment, "You are just like your dad" or "That is something your mother would say" or "I see your wife (or husband) is rubbing off on you." Understand that words and actions are just that, words and actions. What is left are people and the impact they leave. Leave your impact by being the most authentic person you can be. You will be grateful if you do.

Quotes on Values and Authenticity

"Be authentic, be real and be yourself. And the moment you do, your self-esteem will grow by leaps and bounds, and you will unleash a remarkable degree of confidence. You won't even know what is happening, and this will take place at a deep subconscious level. But you will start to see big changes in the way you operate when your social self becomes a mirror reflection of your true self. You will have incredible amounts of energy and you will find you are more creative than ever. You will notice that you have a deep sense of joy and peace within you. Being true to yourself lifts your life to a whole new level and awakens your best self. From a metaphysical viewpoint, when you align your outer world with your inner world, the universe throws its wind beneath your wings and sends you more of its treasures."

Robin Sharma, <u>The Saint, The Surfer, and The CEO</u>

"Time I have only just a minute. Only sixty seconds in it. Forced upon me, can't refuse it. Didn't seek it, didn't choose it. But it's up to me to use it. I must suffer if I lose it. Give accounts if I abuse it. Just a tiny little minute but eternity is in it."
Christine Warren

"You've got to sing like you don't need the money. You have got to love like you'll never get hurt. You've got to dance like there is no one watching. You have got to come from the heart, if you want it to work."
Susanna Clark

"When you fight something, you're tied to it forever. As long as you are fighting it, you are giving it power."
Anthony de Mello

"What you resist persists. And only what you look at, and own, can disappear. You make it disappear by simply changing your mind about it."
Neale Donald Walsch

Chapter 5
Courage

It is not good enough to have a vision and good values. One must act on the vision and move towards realizing their dreams. That is where courage comes in.

You are given the choice: Do you let yourself become a slave to fear, or do you let courage empower you? In order to realize the greatness within yourself and become so much more than you currently are, you need to let courage empower you. Many people have great visions and values but never reach the level of greatness as people like Jesus, Ghandi, Mother Teresa, Buddha, Martin Luther King, Terry Fox, Rick Hansen, and Princess Diana.

The reason many people live the life of mediocrity is because they never grabbed the courage to realize their visions. They were simply nice thoughts in their head. Then someday they see someone on television or in a magazine who took the courage to actually live the dream, the vision that they had before but could not do because they chose fear over courage.

One story of courage near and dear to my heart is the story of when my father found out he had terminal cancer. It was January 1st, 2004 and my father went to the emergency room at the hospital in Calgary for what he thought was a sore back. He had been treated for over two years for what he and the doctors thought was a sore back due to the nature of his work as a heavy duty mechanic. As it turned out it was way worse. After suffering for 3 days and finally not being able to walk, he decided to go get it checked out at the hospital. My sister was in the hospital room with my dad when the doctor returned. Now remember he thought he was going in for a sore back. When the doctor returned he told my father he had some bad news. He proceeded to tell my dad, "The reason for your discomfort Mr. Sigvaldason is a kidney tumour that has grown to the size of a football. You have cancer and it does not look good."

How would you react to news like this? What would you do?

This was my dad's response as my sister broke down in tears beside him. He looked over at her and put his arm around her to comfort her and said, "You know I have lived a great life and if this is God's will then so be it. I will just have to fight hard and make the best out of whatever time I am given."

That is courage! To, in your darkest hour, still be worried more about your loved ones and what they are going through and doing your best to make it easy on them.

My father was a fighter and on many occasions showed what I have termed *"positive stubbornness"* when only given a short while to live. One time that will always be remembered was when he was hospitalized because he could no longer walk and had little energy left. My sister Lisa and brother in law returned from their honeymoon in Europe to tell my dad some great news (a trip they almost cancelled due to my dad's health but he said, "Don't worry I will be here waiting for you when you return... I am not going anywhere soon."). He was going to be a grandfather, an "Afi". This was something he dreamed of and now it was coming true. He decided then and there that he needed to get out of the hospital so he could get better and be there for his grandchild. He literally sprung from his bed and within a few days had willed himself out of the hospital. Although he never lived long enough to see his first grandchild, I know the ultrasound pictures and seeing my sister's belly grow were a source of great joy and comfort in his final months.

Right at the point my father became bed ridden and I was told he would not come out this time; I had a trip to Quebec City planned. It was the Junior Chamber of Commerce national convention and I was to compete in the national effective speaking competition. I didn't want to go for fear something might happen and I would have to return home early or that it would just be on my mind and my concentration would be so far off I wouldn't be able to compete to the best of my abilities. Again my dad was a source of courage and inspiration and said, "Don't worry about me. Nothing is going to happen before your speech. Go give 'em hell son and bring back the title."

I went to Quebec and I did compete. I was determined to do my best and hoped that I would be able to return to Calgary and see my dad one last time and to tell him we did it and I came back with the title. The day of the competition I was focused. My family knew not to contact me unless something serious had happened so as to allow me to focus on the competition as dad had wanted me to do. However, during my speech there were distractions from janitors coming in the hall, doors being left open to the lobby of the hotel and the noise that brings, and no one told me where the timer or the judges were sitting. This threw me a bit but I was determined to get through it and did. However, I went 8 seconds over my time limit which was a huge point deduction – one that normally cannot be overcome. I, along with the other competitors, would have to wait until late that night at the awards banquet to find out the results.

About an hour after the competition I went on a tour with a bunch of the conference delegates to a cookie factory about 45 minutes from Quebec City to take my mind off everything. During the introduction one of the conference organizers got a call on his cell and I got told it was for me. I dreaded this call and knew what it was. My father had passed away about an hour ago with my family by his side and holding his hands. Dad kept his word – nothing did happen before my speech. He waited till I was done to let go of his pain. I felt he was with me while I delivered the speech.

I hurried back and got a ride back to the hotel so I could make arrangements to get back to Calgary as soon as possible. I spent the afternoon on the phone with airline customer service people who helped me book return flights from Quebec to Calgary. I never really had time to think about what had happened.

I was able to book flights out early the Sunday morning so had a day and a half to stay in Quebec City. I was told not to worry about the awards banquet that night since everyone would understand.

I decided not to just sit in my hotel room and wallow in sorrow but rather to go out and support my fellow competitors who were tremendous support and an honour to just be in the same company as.

I sat through the whole dinner and visited with many people from across the country, some of whom made the point to give condolences if they had heard what happened.

I remember one young lady named Courtney Pitcher from Vernon, BC who came up to me to share how my speech had touched her and made a difference to her. She shared with me her story of losing her dad a year earlier. We shed many tears and made a bond that I hope lasts forever. It was at that moment I realized it didn't matter how I did in the competition.

My speech and story made a difference and that is so much more important to me.

After hours of entertainment and a wonderful dinner, the awards ceremony took place. The effective speaking award was the last of the evening. All the competitors were brought to the front for congratulations from the crowd. It felt great just to be up there and sharing in the moment with the soon to be announced winner. Then I heard it. This year's winner of both the Effective Speaking and the Impromptu Speaking Contest is ... Corey Sigvaldason. Emotion overcame me as I tried to hold it together. What a rollercoaster of emotions that day. I had won! All I could think of was "Dad – I gave 'em hell and I am coming home with the title."

I remember growing up always hearing the expression, "Be careful, sometimes you don't know your own strength." This rang true to me when I think of how strong my father was. How unselfish and caring. Sometimes we don't realize our strength and courage. Yet we go forth and dream, dare, and do! *It is at those times when we muster something deep within ourselves that we enter another level of being. A level that is nearly unstoppable and more powerful than any man-made machine. Courage is the engine that makes dreams go!*

Everyone is given choices as we journey through life. We can choose fear or faith. Remember there is no progress without risk. Not until you have a failure can you be sure you aimed high enough. High jumpers keep putting the bar higher and higher until they fail to clear the bar. They don't quit until they fail to clear the bar on at least three attempts. Failure is never 'total' or 'final'. It is only the beginning of your next attempt with new knowledge that will take you to new heights. We are always given another opportunity, another day.

I will bring you back to my question from the beginning of this chapter: *What would you do?*

More Importantly, *What are you going to do?*

I challenge all of you to dare to be your

best and look to the opportunity in your future. Start a crusade in your life. Think of all the possibilities life has to offer you. The only reason you are not already the person you dream of being is that you have not dared to be that person and summoned the courage to pursue the dream.

What are you going to do now?

It is a scientific fact that it isn't so much the head but rather the heart that is the controlling motivator. Let me explain: The heart communicates to the brain through chemicals in the hormonal system. One such chemical in the heart is atrial peptide, a primary driver of motivated behaviour. Stated simply, if we don't *feel* our values and goals, we can't *live* them. It is the heart, not the head, that plays the dominant role in moving us to courage and excellence.

The answers to all your questions lie in your heart, not in your head.

Life is nothing but a long race. We never really know where the finish line is. Yet we run for the sake of running. Put another way, "Life is a series of snapshots – If you don't pay attention to them, you miss out on life."
Corey Sigvaldason

When I think of courage I often think of the serenity prayer; "God grant me the serenity to accept the things I cannot change, courage to change the things I can, and wisdom to know the difference."

Business Philosopher, Peter Koestenbaum links our attitude to courage and was quoted as saying:

> "Some people are more talented than others. Some people are more educationally privileged than others. But we all have the capacity to be great. Greatness comes by recognizing that your potential is limited only by how you choose, how you use your freedom, how resolute you are, how persistent you are – in short, by your attitude. And we are all free to choose our attitude."

In addition to attitude I have found laughter can truly be the best medicine. In fact, I love what Robin Williams says in the movie *Patch Adams*:

> "The American Journal of Medicine has found that laughter increases secretion of catecholamines and endorphins which in turn increases oxygenation of the blood, relaxes the arteries, speeds the heart, decreases blood pressure, which has a positive effect on all cardiovascular and respiratory ailments as well as increasing the immune system response."

I know in preparing to give presentations or a speech I always smile lots beforehand and during. The simple act of smiling lifts spirits, shows confidence, and actually makes one feel better and more confident.

Introductory psychology tells of the concept of stimulus and response. What I think is missing or, if it has not since been added to textbooks, is the idea of choice. In particular, the choice, or freedom to choose, the response given to any stimulus.

STIMILUS → FREEDOM TO CHOOSE → RESPONSE

The day before I wrote this I was at a funeral for a thirty year old man I just met through my church. He wrote a piece on life choices that was on the back of the card for his service that I feel is appropriate for this talk. It was called *Life Choices:*

"Most people do not realize just how precious life really is.

I myself have taken it for granted far too often.

I have made choices with no regard for those who care for and love me.

I have been selfish in the past.

Taken the wrong path far too often.

Not because of mis-direction but because of poor choices.

Though no one thing do I regret.

The choices I have made for myself,

Have built the character within me today.

I am who I am because of the choices both good and bad.

I would not give up who I am today for anything.

I may get sad, mad, or depressed,

But I have to forge through to what awaits.

By that I mean what is meant for me.

All these choices in life I have made

Will help me become a better stronger person.

People say you learn from your mistakes.

I think we all learn from the choices we make.

Written by Caelin William Bond Smith (1977-2007)

Caelin really puts this in perspective nicely. If you ever had the opportunity to meet him or see him, you know he was one of the most authentic individuals you will ever meet and had no problem standing out from the crowd. Whether it was coloured hair or shaved head and lots of tattoos Caelin was always as unique as he was authentic. Caelin will be missed but his legacy will continue to grow.

Just as Caelin and others have come to realize, you are not a pawn in the game of life. Every stimulus, event, or circumstance does not determine your path in life. Rather, you have the freedom to choose your response. Robin Sharma puts it this way; ***"circumstances don't define a person, they reveal a person."*** I recently attended a workshop that taught me even more about choice and that not only do we choose our responses but we also choose our stimulus. It takes the idea of choice to a new level I want you all to consider since then everything in our lives is a result of choice if that is the case. Think back to my father's response to the news of his terminal cancer. The news he received was the stimulus and he had many choices in how to respond. It was in his freedom to choose that his response was so profound and left a legacy to the many people who knew him and heard his story. I challenge you to choose responses that make a difference in your life and leave a positive impact in the world. When you do, not only will you find courage but you will inspire others to do the same and you will be leaving a positive legacy.

Courage Quotes

Edmond Burke:

> "The battle of life in most cases is fought up hill and to win it without a struggle is almost like winning it

without honour. If there were no difficulties, there would be no successes; if there were nothing to struggle for, there would be nothing to be achieved. Difficulties may intimidate the weak, but they act only as a wholesome stimulus to men of resolution and valour. All experiences of life, indeed, serves to prove that the impediments thrown in the way of human advancement may, for the most part, be overcome by steady good conduct, honest zeal, activity, perseverance, and, above all, by a determined resolution to surmount difficulties and to stand up manfully against misfortune."

Theodore Roosevelt:

"It is not the critic that counts; not the man who points out how the strongman stumbled or where the doer of the deeds could have done better. The credit belongs to the man who is actually in the arena; who strives valiantly, who errs and comes short again and again, because there is no effort without error and shortcoming; who does actually try to do the deed; who knows the great enthusiasm, the great devotion, knows in the end the triumph of great achievement, and who, at worst, if he fails, at least fails while daring greatly. *Far better it is to dare mighty things, to win glorious triumphs even though checkered by failure, than to rank with those poor spirits who neither enjoy nor suffer much because they live in the grey twilight that knows neither victory nor defeat."*

Andrew Carnegie:
"As I get older I pay less attention to what men and women say but I pay attention to what they do."

Peter Legge in his book <u>Who Dares Win</u> says this:

"I challenge you to start a crusade in your life-To dare to be your best. Think of the possibilities. The only reason you are not the person you should be is that you don't dare to be that person. *Once you dare, once you stop drifting with the crowd and face life courageously, life takes on a new significance,* and new forces take shape within you.

Robin Sharma in <u>The Saint, The Surfer, and The CEO</u> says this:

> "A mistake is only a mistake if you repeat it. The first time, it's nothing more than a beautiful lesson."

Chapter 6
One Person Making A Difference

Another key to living your life of purpose lies in realizing that one person can make a difference. Each person is like a drop of water in the ocean, a small, seemingly insignificant part of the larger ocean. However, a drop of water creates a ripple effect that can spread. It is a statistical fact that one drop of water changes the chemical composition of the whole entire ocean and changes it forever. Nothing, now matter how small or seemingly insignificant, is without impact in this world.

The graphic below shows how we all have a value center in the middle of our circle of influence. Our values come from a variety of sources but they reflect what is core to us. From there we spread our impact through our circle of influence like the ripple effect in the ocean, changing the world forever. Everyone contributes and everyone is significant! It is through the circle of influence and the impact we make that a legacy ripple starts and continues, often long after we leave this world.

To illustrate the impact just one person can have in the world I will point you to the following historical facts on the importance of the power of one:

1) One more vote and Andrew Jackson would've been impeached

2) One more vote in 1645 gave Oliver Cromwell control of England

3) One more vote by a cancer stricken farmer who rode from New Jersey to Philadelphia in a driving hailstorm to cast a vote, made the Declaration Of Independence a unanimously supported document.

4) One vote in 1875 changed France from a monarchy to a republic

5) One more vote in every precinct in Chicago and JFK would not have been president of the US

One story near and dear to my heart of one person making a difference is the story of my grade 10 science class substitute teacher – Sue Veillette. She literally changed the course of my life. I was struggling in school and had major behavioural issues at the time. It was the last class of the day and I had a substitute so I was at my worst. Miss Veillette asked me to stay after class for a minute and proceeded to tell me that she saw something in me that day that she wanted to share. She said I showed signs of brilliance when asked questions and that I knew my material and that I could easily be the best student in the class. It was only my behaviour that led to bad marks. She gave me hope and empowered me that day to change my life - and I did. By the end of that year, I was an honour roll student and went on to build a successful business of my own. It was that day I realized I could do or become anything I wanted. Teachers are in the business of educating our future leaders and Sue showed how teachers can make a difference.

The best way to make a difference is by leading with your heart. Your heart knows and always does best. It is by leading with your heart that you are content with who you are being and becoming.

I had a great example in my life of a businessman who led with his heart and made a difference in my life. Kirk Ba-ethke (a.k.a. Kirk Fraser, the voice of the Blazers) who was working in the head office for the Kamloops Blazers hockey franchise went over and above his job description and led by heart. I had set up a tour for my terminally ill dad to go down and meet the coaches and see the office and locker room while he was visiting me. However, the day I was suppose to take my dad, he was very ill from his cancer and could not make it. I had asked if I could come in and grab a jersey and was told that the store was closed. What Kirk did next will stay with me the rest of my life. Somehow he managed to get a game worn jersey and called me back to tell me to come by and pick it up. Before my dad left to go home I was able to give him that jersey and I will never forget the smile it put on his face in his time of pain. Shortly after, my father went into the hospital and that jersey was the only thing he took in the hospital with him. Kirk not only led by his heart but touched the hearts of many through that act and that to me is the essence of making a difference.

When you have vision, courage, and lead with your heart, YOU MAKE A DIFFERENCE.

I challenge you to think about the differences you are already making and have made in the world. Think of all the great things you have done, are doing, and will do in the future. Then think about how your actions touch the lives of those around you and your circle of influence and the potential for that to multiply through the effect you have on others. When you do, you will see your contribution (your drop of water in the ocean of life) creates a legacy ripple which has and will continue to change the world forever.

Chapter 7
Love

Fulfillment in life does not come from collecting more things, driving fancy cars, or living in huge homes. It comes from giving and receiving more love. The Beatles sang "The love you take is the love you make." When you feel unloved, and I know there are times it happens, my suggestion to you is give more love.

As Gary Chapman says in his book <u>The Five Love Languages</u>, we need to constantly be filling our love tanks. It is when our love tanks are low (like gas in a car) that we need to fill it. We fill it by giving and showing love. In turn our tank fills as others show love to us. Stop at every station in life and do your best to keep your love tank full.

When you just can't seem to see love in your life, be a beacon of love and show more love. Rather than searching harder and racing and worrying when you will ever find love just show love. Love attracts love. Love is like a mirror, it reflects back what you give it. Love abounds and is always there.

When someone you love really hurts you to your core, try showing them love and compassion. This disarms their hurt and you can feel comfortable and at peace with yourself. I am not talking about being a pushover or a mat. Love is the biggest band-aid.

"Real love begins where nothing is expected in return" **Antoine De Saint-Exupery**

My favourite writing on Love is from the Bible in 1 Corinthians 13. This is commonly referred to as the love chapter. Although nearly two thousand years old, there is a reason why this is the most quoted source on love, it truly captures the essence of love. It is used at many weddings, which are a pinnacle expressions for love in its truest form. Here is what it says:

"If I speak in human and angelic tongues but do not have love, I am a resounding gong or a clashing cymbal. And if I have the gift of prophecy and comprehend all mysteries and knowledge; if I have all faith so as to move mountains but do not have love, I am nothing. If I give away everything I own to feed the poor, and if I hand my body over so that I may boast but do not have love, I gain nothing.

Love is patient, love is kind. It is not jealous, love does not brag and is not arrogant. It is not rude, it does not seek its own interests, it is not quick-tempered, it does not brood over injury. It does not rejoice over wrongdoing but rejoices over the truth. It bears all things, believes all things, hopes all things, endures all things. Love never fails.

If there are prophecies, they will be brought to nothing; if tongues, they will cease; if knowledge, it will be brought to nothing. For we know partially and we prophesy partially, but when the perfect comes, the partial will pass away. When I was a child, I used to talk as a child, think as a child, reason as a child; when

I became a man, I put aside child-ish things. At present we see indis-tinctly, as in a mirror, but then face to face. At present I know partially; then I shall know fully, as I am fully known.

So faith, hope, and love remain, but the greatest of these is love (1)."

I would summarize this writing this way: Without love, faith is cold and dor-mant. Without love, hope is grim. Love is the fire that kindles hope and the light which turns faith into certainty.

Love is inspiring. The word 'inspire' actually means "to breathe the breath of life into." With the experience of being with my mother and father when they were dying, I have come to a greater clarity on the meaning and purpose of life.

When I sat down with my parents and we talked about serious issues many in-sights came to me. I remember one con-versation with my dad before he died that will forever stick with me. The topic was "Are you ready to die?" Often people will say, what do you mean? Do you mean fi-nancially? Or some other situation like that? I answer, "No, I mean spiritually." Are you spiritually ready to die? Because *until you are ready to die, you truly cannot live."* That is one of the greatest paradoxes of life…that until you are ready to die, you really cannot live. Many different spiritual philosophies and religions have this as a core value in their beliefs.

In my life I have been blessed to have many people I love and who love me. However, it wasn't until I met my wife Angela (I think of her as my Angel-a) that I truly understood love. It was after meeting her I realized that the Beatles were not only great musicians but also great philosophers with their insight. It is true – love is all you need!

Before meeting her and having the spiritual awakening I went through, I was success chasing. My priorities were wrong and I lived a life disconnected. I hurt many people along the way in my selfish quest for power, prestige, promotions, material possessions, self-indulgence, and unimportant 'stuff'. I blamed everyone and everything around me for my problems and setbacks. Very seldom did I take responsibility and accountability. I put all my worth in external forces which I had little to no control over. However, God, the universe, the creator, or whomever you believe to be a higher power than us, has a way of humbling us and bringing us back down to our reality. Some choose to argue with reality. However, the fact remains, if you do argue with reality, it will be a lifelong struggle that can never be won until you accept reality. My coach Richard Burley says, "unless you go within, you will go without!"

I met my wife Angela after what was the most trying two and a half years of my life. I lost my father, mother, first wife, and business. I was in a downward spiral. Faith was there but cold. Hope was grim. At the time I did not realize I was surrounded by love. Instead, I was under my own pile of manure and kept shovelling more on. I was blinded by my own self-pity and excuses which kept me from allowing the best the world had to offer. With the help of my faith, family and true friends, I got back in the game and accepted my current state and surrendered to my higher power and what He has planned for my life. It was only then that it came together for me.

I use to think that I would only be loved or accepted if I made a certain sum of money, held a position, and accomplished many things. The reality is none of that truly matters and can be snapped away in a heartbeat. At the end of the day, it is our love and relationships that matter the most to us. After being in intensive care of the hospital a number of times, I never saw anyone bring in a fancy car, a medal they won, or their work to finish. Rather, all they wanted and needed was to have loved ones by their side. It is when we see the difference that loved ones make in our lives and our impact on them that our purpose is crystal clear – love is all we need!

Now I know and understand this love through the relationship with my wife. Until I met her, love was a warm fuzzy feeling that came to me from time to time. I am sure I have had love like this before but I was blinded to it and it took meeting my soul mate to have my eyes opened and for my priorities to become crystal clear. With true love, your loved one knows all your faults and irritating habits and *chooses* to love you anyway. *Love is work* but it is the best work in life.

I have had some great role models of love in my life. In particular, my mother and stepfather have been inspirational when it comes to love. I will preface this by saying I am a lot like my mother in many ways and this can be trying for those loved ones around us. However, my stepfather never let difficult or even highly unlikely waver his commitment and love for my mother.

To prove the point, he stayed with my mother and their love actually grew into something more beautiful than anything I have ever seen after the accident that left her a quadriplegic.

Statistically, over eighty percent of marriages end in divorce under the circumstances they faced. I know many people have said to my stepfather "I don't know how you do it Frank. It seems like so much work and commitment."

Now remember what I said about love and work – love is work but it is the best work in life. Many people, including myself, call my stepfather an angel on earth. When I had a conversation recently with my stepfather and discussed this, what he said blew me away and made it all make sense. He said, "Your mother was the angel. She was my inspiration and made loving her so easy. Anything I had to do was minor compared to what she went through each and every day. It never felt like work or even difficult. You just do things for your loved ones out of love. When you do, it is never work. I just wish I could have done more."

That is love and commitment.

I remember talking with mom before she passed away and asked her what her favourite moments were. She said, "Just when dad and I are lying beside each other and watching a movie and he is holding my hand. The other time is when I see him walk through the door every day after coming home from work." I also know she loved that he would always kiss her twice before going to work each day.

It is the little things done on a consistent basis that make a difference. It is never about the lifestyle you lead or what you bought last year for a birthday. It is the little things (kisses, hugs, holding hands, spending time together, saying "I love you", the love you give and receive) that are the big things.

I hope you understand the importance of being rich before being wealthy. Being rich is the realization that you have everything you already need and appreciate and love to the fullest.

At the end of our lives we look at those we love and the relationships we made. On death's door our priorities come to us with unusual clarity. If given the chance we tell all those people who made a difference, or who we loved, or loved us, what they mean in our lives. My question to all of you is *why wait?* Use every opportunity you have to tell someone the difference they make in your life and how much you love them. Tell them how proud you are and thankful that they are part of your life. Many people can travel through life with regrets but I assure you this act will be something you never regret. The only regret may be not doing it sooner.

Love Them Anyway

People are unreasonable, illogical and self-centered.
Love them anyway.

If you are kind, people may accuse you of selfish ulterior motives.
Be kind anyway.

If you are successful, you will win some false friends and true enemies.
Succeed anyway.

The good you do today will be forgotten tomorrow.
Be good anyway.

Honesty and frankness will make you vulnerable.
Be honest and frank anyway.

What you spend years building may be destroyed overnight.
Build anyway.

In the final analysis, it is between you and God.
It was never between you and them anyway.

Mother Theresa

Chapter 8
Conclusion

In the final analysis, the key to immor-tality and success in life is the *Reassur-ance that our lives mattered and were not lived in vain.*

I would commend to you the words of Ralph Waldo Emerson:

> "To laugh often and much, to win the respect of intelligent people and the affection of children, to earn the appreciation of honest critics and en-dure the betrayal of false friends; to appreciate beauty to find the best in others; to leave the world a bit better whether by a healthy child, a garden

patch or a redeemed social condition, to know that even one life has breathed easier because you lived. This is to have succeeded."

Before I finish I want to share with you the last conversation I had with my dad before he died. In it I share with him what he taught me in his lifetime.

What my Father Taught Me In His Lifetime

1) Unconditional Love

2) Authenticity – More people need this

3) Generosity

4) Family as a cornerstone

5) Live In The Now

6) Appreciate all the blessings in our lives – "It's about what we have, not what we don't have or need to get"

7) Strength

8) Caring and compassion

9) Unselfishness

10) The value of a photo – some say a picture is worth a thousand words. I say a picture is worth way more. It represents a shared moment. A snapshot in time. It is the only tangible way to capture time. To get it back.

11) Value of having a strong financial house in order

12) Value of our health

13) Teamwork (Value of sports)

14) Even when we are apart, you are always in my heart.

"You have been an amazing father, husband, brother, son, uncle, and friend to so many. I am so, SO proud to call you dad! I will always remember the lessons you have taught me. You are an inspiration to all those that meet you. I know there will come a day when you are no longer here but realize your legacy has made an impact in this world and will last forever and be past on through many generations to come. I love you so much dad and I hate to say goodbye. I am going to miss you so much even though I will talk with you everyday. I love you." We then exchanged a hug and kiss and he said this to me, "I love you and I am so proud of you." I don't believe there is anything better or needed to say to a person than that. *I encourage all of you to call someone you love and tell them how much you love them and how proud you are of them.*

Do not put off living any longer. Life fulfillment comes not from accumulating things but from what the famous psychologist Abraham Maslow calls self-actualization. Happiness in life does not come from getting, it comes from giving and you do that just by being. So stop playing the game of "keeping up with the Joneses" or "the one with the most wins." Stop trying to take more from life and be more for life. That is where true happiness lies and the richness of the world reveals itself to you.

"I expect to pass through this life but once. If therefore there be any kindness I can show, or any good thing I can do to any fellow being, let me do it now, and not defer or neglect it, as I shall not pass this way again."

William Penn

Go forth and live your lives like it may be your last day and know you are all successes and already have it all. Remember having it all does not necessarily mean having it all at once.

September 11, 2001, while stuck in the World Trade Center during the attacks, nobody worried about the work in their office. Nobody called their broker or looked over the internet at the value of their investments. Everyone, without exception, called his or her family. Almost universally, their last words were, "If I don't make it out of here alive, I just want you to know I love you and the kids."

Nothing matters more to us than the people we love. Not jobs, not investments, not our plans for the future.

"The most reliable way to matter to the world is to love those closest to us, our mates, our children, our families, our closest friends."

Corey Sigvaldason

Harold Kushner in his book <u>Living a Life That Matters</u> puts it this way:

> *"Our love changes them even as the ability to love changes us, even as our inviting and accepting their love changes them and changes us as well.... Do we yearn to matter to the world? We matter, not because of our achievements but because we are loved by God and loved by people around us. That love may not shield us from pain, death, and loss, but it will make them more bearable, and that will be enough."*

Another of my favourite authors, Mitch Albom says this in his book <u>Tuesdays With Morrie</u>:

"As long as we can love each other, and remember the feeling of love we had, we can die without ever really going away. All the love you created is still there. All the memories are still there. You live on – in the hearts of everyone you have touched and nurtured while you were here.... Death ends a life, not a relationship."

We don't always have to cram in as much as we can in each and every day. I agree we need to make the most of every day but that does not necessarily mean doing or saying a lot. In life, sometimes the little things are the big things. The success you all seek and experience comes down to the choices you make each and every minute and every hour of your life. I know through talking with many loved ones and family who have lost loved ones, they all say that when sick or facing hardships the most important thing for them was just holding their loved ones hand and rubbing it. Quite literally, the biggest part is just showing up - just being there. Many have shared with me that saying and hearing, "I love you" makes all the difference. Knowing at the end of it all that you made a difference in this world.

Your legacy lives on and you did matter and had tremendous success and impact.

Robin Sharma in <u>The Saint, Surfer, and CEO</u> has this to say:

> *"Remember that on your deathbed, you'll never regret having been the most loving person you knew or having been someone who trusted people and showered them with unconditional love. Actually, at the end of your life, you just might find that was the best, most fulfilling thing you ever did. By growing more deliberate and intentional in terms of the amount of love and kindness you deliver to other people, you'll strengthen your heart.*

> *The deepest need of the human heart is the need to live for something higher than ourselves. We all have a deep craving to show up in the world in a way that makes a difference in the lives of others and connects us with a purpose that transcends the boundaries of our lives. We all have a human hunger to know at the end of our lives that we haven't walked*

the planet in vain."

"Begin with the end in mind" is the phrase popularized by Steven Covey. In Epitaph Theory, I take this to the extreme and ask you to look at the end of your life and work backwards while moving forward to your beautiful future.

Even though you are never given a deadline for your time on this Earth, I believe you realize you can't live forever. Everyone is given a finite time to accomplish their goals, dreams, and visions but the legacy and impact on the world can last forever.

I challenge all of you to live your life like you are writing your own epitaph. Be remembered for what you did as well as who you are. Choose today to start building your legacy!

Back Material

Other Books

- Corey has one other book out that he co-authored with his aunt Bonnie Breton. The book is a children's book called "No-Leap Webfoot." It is an inspirational book that speaks to the hero in each of us. It combines a well written story with the world class illustrations of William McAusland.

Coaching

- One of Corey's passions is working with small to medium sized businesses and professionals with his personalized coaching program. For more details on how Corey can empower you to get to the next level of success or just find more balance in your busy life, check out his website for further details.

Speaking

- In conjunction with this book, Corey developed a Keynote speech called "Epitaph Theory." It is a speech he developed and used in his quest to win the Canadian Junior Chamber of Commerce Effective Speaking Competition in 2004.

Corporate Training

- The most popular programs that Corey delivers are "The Language of Leadership," "Accelerating Word Of Mouth Marketing," and "Selling Without Smelling." Corey also offers personalized training to meet the needs or you or your company and such training ranges from team building to public speaking and presentation skills.

Business Consulting

- Corey's background as an entrepreneur, manager, and university instructor make him sought after by many companies and individuals looking to make significant breakthroughs in performance, markets, and profits. He brings experience in marketing, strategic management, operations management, office procedures, organizational behaviour, human resources, branding, and international business.

For more information and contact information on any of the above can be found at Corey's website:

http://www.strategicpartners.ca

Endnotes

Introduction

1. Robin Sharma, Who Will Cry When You Die? Life Lessons From The Monk Who Sold His Ferrari, (Toronto, Harper Collins Publishers Ltd., 1999)

Chapter 2 - Success

1. Robin Sharma, The Saint, The Surfer, and The CEO, (Carlsbad, CA., Hay House Inc., 2003), pp 195-1966

Chapter 7 - Love

The Bible, 1 Corinthians 13:1-13

About The Author

Corey has been an entrepreneur since the age of 10 and it is still a passion to this day. Businesses he owned range from; a landscaping company, contracting company, publishing company, financial services firm, to corporate training and business consulting/coaching. He is a national speaking champion and was runner up in an international competition in Brazil in 2005.

Corey has always been very active in community organizations wherever he lived and has been involved with organizations ranging from the Chamber of Commerce and Junior Chamber International, Rotary, Toastmasters, multiple networking groups, church organizations, youth organizations, and many more.

Corey moved on from his entrepreneur lifestyle in 2006 to successfully obtain an MBA at Thompson Rivers University. Showing his spirit of entrepreneurship and business sense during his studies, landed him a position working for TRU as an Assistant to the Dean in the School of Business and as an Instructor which eventually sent him to India in 2008 for TRU World where he taught a Post-Baccalaureate in Marketing. He has also taught in Manitoba, specifically with First Nation students.

Corey brings with him a strong background in training and finance and has extensive experience as an entrepreneur which have benefited hundreds of companies and individuals he has helped. He has personally been involved in business successorship a number of times and knows firsthand the challenges involved and looks forward to helping clients with planning for successful transition of their businesses.